# JavaScript:

# Learn JavaScript In 24 Hours Or Less

## *A Beginner's Guide To Learning JavaScript Programming Now*

# Table Of Contents

Introduction ................................................................. 5

Chapter 1: HTML Overview .......................................... 8

Choosing a Text Editor ................................................. 8

Choosing a Web Browser ............................................ 10

What is HTML? ............................................................ 11

Chapter 2: Introduction to JavaScript ........................ 16

Piecing Together HTML and JavaScript .................... 16

a. Internal JavaScript ................................................. 17

b. External JavaScript ................................................ 18

c. Instant JavaScript .................................................. 19

Meet JavaScript ........................................................... 19

Storing Information .................................................... 23

Chapter 3: JavaScript Essentials ................................. 25

Data Types ................................................................... 26

Knowing what the Interpreter is Thinking ............... 29

Flow Control ............................................................... 30

If Statement ................................................................ 32

Debugging ................................................................... 37

What to look for when debugging: ................................................ 40

Recap ............................................................................................ 41

Chapter 4: Functions and Data Manipulation ........................... 43

Mathematical Precedence .......................................................... 44

A new contender: modulo .......................................................... 46

Messing with strings ................................................................... 49

Functions ..................................................................................... 51

Return Values ............................................................................. 55

Optimisation: Finding the Perfect Balance Between Readability and Conciseness .......................................................................... 57

Global and Local Variables ........................................................ 59

Chapter 5: Loops and Arrays ..................................................... 62

For-Loops .................................................................................... 63

Arrays ........................................................................................... 66

A Mini Project: Text-Searching ................................................. 73

Still Confused? ............................................................................ 78

Chapter 6: Mastering Flow Control .......................................... 80

While Loops ................................................................................ 80

Do-While Loops ......................................................................... 85

If-Else If-Else .............................................................................. 87

Switch Statement ........................................................................ 89

Review .......................................................................................... 91

Chapter 7: Managing Data More Efficiently ................................. 99

Arrays - A Quick Review ................................................................. 99

Two-Dimensional Arrays ............................................................... 101

Introduction to Objects ................................................................. 103

Custom Constructors ..................................................................... 113

Chapter 8: Exploring Objects ....................................................... 116

Identifying Data Types .................................................................. 116

Distinguishing Between Different Objects .............................. 117

Data Verification ............................................................................ 119

Running through properties in a loop ....................................... 121

Conclusion ....................................................................................... 125

# Introduction

The Internet has come a long way since the early 90's. With hundreds of thousands of computers already connected in a network, there arose the dilemma as to how data were to be distributed to different computers in an organized manner. With this in mind, Tim Berners-Lee created a hyperlinking framework known as the Hypertext Transfer Protocol (HTTP). Alongside HTTP he also created a markup language known as the Hypertext Markup Language (HTML).

In modern web browsers, most of the time you no longer have to type in HTTP or HTTPS in order to visit a website. You also won't see the .html extension very often as you surf the web. These are done in order to simplify the web browsing experience for casual users.

As you may have noticed, there's a trend among web developers to make things as simple as possible for the web surfers. While the early 2000's seemed good enough for a lot of people, with the advent of flashy, glossy text and buttons and "click here to enter" flash intros, these elements do not accurately represent the current trend of minimalist, dynamic content. The old sites required you to load and reload different web pages whenever you click a button, which hampers the web surfing experience, as a lot of data would get lost in data fields because you had to keep refreshing web pages to check for updated content. In short, as information grew more dense and complex, there was a need to simplify how we access those bits and pieces of information, otherwise we end up drowning in a sea of data.

This book isn't a reference guide, nor is it a set of dry academic lectures; it's a practical walkthrough in JavaScript programming, built on the very idea current web technologies are built upon - the need to simplify.

Before going any further, ask yourself these questions:

- Do you have a computer that has a functional browser and an internet connection?

- Do you want to learn how to create web pages that can intelligently talk balk to the user and add new information in real time?

- Do you prefer friendly walkthroughs over dull and dry reference manuals?

If you've answered yes to at least number 2 and 3, this book is for you. In case you've answered no to number 1, you may want to consider getting Google Chrome or Mozilla Firefox, both of which are excellent browsers, to start you off, otherwise the sample codes may not work as intended.

Note:

If you truly wish to learn as quickly as you can from this book, then I advise doing ALL the exercises and activities in the chapters. Resist the urge to skim through sample codes without trying them out yourself - running the codes help you understand and apply what you've learned. Speed-reading through the chapters will only give you surface-level knowledge - enough to impress programming novices at a dinner party.

Let's begin the journey.

# Chapter 1: HTML Overview

HTML, CSS, and Javascript work in tandem to give users a seamless web experience. A lot of budding web developers have these three confused. If you're completely new to the world of web development, this chapter should give you a quick tour of HTML. On the other hand, if you already know HTML, feel free to skip or skim this chapter.

**Choosing a Text Editor**

Before you start creating interactive webpages, you'll have to download a good text editor. While Macs and PCs usually have built-in text editors that can save files in html format, they lack a lot of useful utilities that make web development a lot easier like syntax highlighting and auto-completion. That being said, here are some of the best text editors for web development:

1. Atom – Atom is a relatively new text editor by Github. It's free, open source, and has plenty of customization options. Basically, Atom is like a programmable text editor; it can do almost anything you want it to with the right plug-ins. Among its many features would be the Fuzzy finder, which allows you to jump to different files with a simple cmd+t command, and the wide range of available themes. It works on Mac OS X, Windows, and Linux and comes at no cost, so try it out and see if suits you.

2. Sublime Text – Sublime Text is quite aptly named, as it offers a sublime writing experience due to its intuitive commands and beautiful interface. Like Atom, Sublime Text is also highly customizable and works on Mac OSX, Windows, and Linux. Its trial version is free, but the full version costs about $70.

3. Notepad++ - Notepad++ has been a crowd favorite for quite some time because of its unrivaled simplicity and speed. If you just need a no-nonsense text editor that'll let you edit a couple of html files without the need for complex file structures, you may opt to give this text editor a try. Keep in mind, however, that this text editor is only available in Windows.

4. Brackets – Brackets is quite a unique text editor from Adobe, as it's designed to work in tandem with Adobe's other products, specifically Photoshop. If you're interested in creating sleek user interfaces from Photoshop, Brackets allows you to extract information seamlessly from the PSDs you've created and convert them into CSS code. This text editor works with Windows, Linux, and Mac OSX, so if you're interested in web design, you'll want to have this installed in your system.

If you're not trying to save space on your system, I recommend downloading these four text editors and trying them out for yourself, assuming that you're running a compatible operating system. The exercises and code snippets in this book do not require a specific text editor so feel free to jump in and out of different text editors until you find one that fits your needs.

## Choosing a Web Browser

Text editors allow you to create and save html files while web browsers allow you to view them. Unfortunately, sometimes, the web pages you create may look and act differently when viewed on different browsers, so here are the browsers you'll want installed on your system:

- Google Chrome – Google Chrome is one of the most popular web browsers because of its speed and simplicity. With its built-in developer tools you get to play around with the web sites you build and change snippets of code on the fly so you can immediately see what lines of code you'll want to change.

- Firefox – Firefox comes with a plug-in called Firebug, which somewhat functions like Google Chrome's developer tools. It also comes with a mobile preview mode, which basically allows you to see how your website would look when viewed in a mobile device.

- Internet explorer – this isn't something you can install on Linux or Mac OSX and in Windows this comes preinstalled, however, if you are running Windows you'll want to test your html code using this browser as well, simply because it often messes up configurations that worked on Google Chrome or Firefox.

- Vivaldi - a relatively new contender, the first beta was launched only in 2015, with the first stable release launched in 2016. The reason why this browser made it in this list is because it's made based on modern web technologies such as HTML5 and Node.js among other things. It also runs on Mac, Windows, and Linux, so if you're looking for a new, cutting edge browser, give this one a try.

## What is HTML?

HTML basically allows you to present your site's content in a structured manner. Think of it as a blueprint for building a house; it tells you where the living room, bathroom, kitchen, and other rooms will be placed and how they harmoniously interconnect.

Learning the structure of an HTML file is quite simple; it's structured almost like an essay - you provide a title, a skeletal structure, and content that flows coherently within the structure. Whenever you read an article, the title tells you what the article talks about, and the content is structured in a particular way, oftentimes with a sentence that piques your interest, followed by anecdotes, facts and figures, arguments, and a conclusion. When you start coding in HTML, you'll see how similarly structured it is to articles you read or write.

Creating an HTML file, then, is as simple as saving your file with a .html file extension. When you create documents in a word processor like Microsoft Word, you'll notice that when you save your file it has either an .odt, .doc, .docx, or something similar at the end of the filename. This tells the computer to read and format the contents of the file in a very specific way. This is because whenever you save something you've created using a word processor you're not just saving a bunch of words you've typed; you're also saving the font size, font styles, and other formatting styles you've used so that when you open your file, your computer will check the file extension, read the contents according to the file extension specified, and then present you the file you've created, making sure that it looks exactly the same way when you've saved it.

HTML basically acts the same way, but this time you use tags in order to tell the computer what to do with the data enclosed by the tags; this allows you to easily change the font styles and other aspects of your web page. Think of HTML as a more precise version of a Word Document. For example, take a look at the text below:

This is a sentence.

If you save this as a Word Document, it will save not only the text, but also its font style, size, and structure. The attributes of the document you've just saved is tucked neatly inside the file and accessible only through the word processor menus. However, if you want to display the same sentence in HTML form, the HTML file would look like this:

```
<html>
  <head>
  </head>
  <body>
    <p>This is a sentence.</p>
```

```
</body>
</html>
```

By saving this file with a .html extension, you get a basic webpage that displays "This is a sentence." Notice how it has the same string of text as the previous text box, but it contains additional tags you may or may not be familiar with. When your browser opens this file, it understands the tags and displays only the content on the previous text box; it doesn't actually show the tags to the user. The most basic tags are shown in the code example:

- The <html> tag - contains everything in your web page. It's the alpha and the omega, literally; never forget the <html> tag or else your site won't work properly!

- The <head> tag - keeps the title and other preliminary scripts that the body might use. For instance, if you want to use a set of design protocols (typically in the form of CSS) that dictate what type of fonts to use, their colors, etc., you can place the code or its reference here.

- The <body> tag - this is where your content goes. From text, to sound, to images, to videos, this is where everything happens.

Don't worry too much if you don't yet fully understand how these tags work; you'll learn better how they work by trying them out in future sample codes and exercises.

## HTML Essentials

Now that you have a general overview of how HTML works, we're going to have a quick run through the basics, just enough to help you learn how to integrate JavaScript seamlessly into it.

We've discussed how HTML files are like Word Documents with additional tags, so let's start with a simple line of text. Type this into your text editor:

> Hi There!

Now create a folder in your computer where you can store all the html files are created and save what you've just typed with a .html extension (e.g., "My First Website.html"). A standard practice for programmers is to create a folder called 'Developer' -- this is where all your files that pertain to programming are stored. You can place this in your home folder. Inside the Developer folder, create a folder called 'Web Development' and for now, place all your html files here. If you're using TextEdit or other text editors that aren't built specifically for html files, remember to check the settings and make sure that "Plain text" format is selected.

Now that you've created your first html file, open it using any web browser you have and see a simple string of text appear before your very eyes! Notice, however, that what you've typed into the text editor (referred to as "source code") looks just like what the browser displayed; it didn't have the <html> tags and other stuff. What gives?

Now, try changing your html file by adding a few tags. It should then look like this:

```
<!DOCTYPE html>
<html>
  <body>
    Hi There!
  </body>
</html>
```

Now reload your browser and see what happens.

Your browser isn't malfunctioning; the web page looks pretty much the same despite the addition of tags in the source code. At this point you may not fully understand why tags are used, but don't worry; you'll see what they're for when you start programming in HTML more.

## Conclusion

You've just had your first dive into HTML- nothing too thorough, just enough of the basics to help you use JavaScript with HTML properly. If you're interested in learning more about HTML, you'll want to take a look at online tutorials and references, as well as see how other web developers code their own sites. You can do the latter by right-clicking a site and clicking on 'view page source' or something along those lines. If you're ready to take the plunge into JavaScript, head over to chapter 2.

# Chapter 2: Introduction to JavaScript

Now that we've covered the essentials of HTML, we can now introduce the basics of programming, with JavaScript as the medium. Make sure that you at least understand the backbone of HTML before proceeding, otherwise, feel free to go back to Chapter 1 and skim through the material once more.

**Piecing Together HTML and JavaScript**

JavaScript conveniently fits into HTML quite readily using the script tag. The script tag can either contain a JavaScript code or a reference to a .js file that contains the JavaScript code. The latter is advised when creating long JavaScript code to avoid mixing up different programming languages in one file - that'd be like writing an essay with some paragraphs in English and some paragraphs in Latin! Internal JavaScript is, however, good to use when you're testing out small fragments of JavaScript code.

## a. Internal JavaScript

If you want to use JavaScript without having to create a .js file, you can simply put the JavaScript inside the script tag as shown below:

```
<script>
  alert("Hi There!");
</script>
```

Put this inside your HTML file as show below and check out your first JavaScript code popping-up to greet you!

```
<!DOCTYPE html>
<html>
  <body>
    <script>
      alert("Hi There!");
    </script>
  </body>
</html>
```

Pretty cool, huh? While this chunk of code is simple enough to understand, when you begin writing websites with more complex codes, keeping different programming/scripting languages in one file becomes rather unwieldy. It makes sense to place the JavaScript code in a separate file so that the HTML code stays neat and easier to maintain. This is where external JavaScript comes in.

**b. External JavaScript**

Just as you can reference a CSS file from an HTML file to keep the codes separate, you can also keep JavaScript in a separate file and simply reference that file from HTML. In order to use JavaScript code saved in another file, you'll simply have to use a script tag that contains an src attribute that references the file you'd like to use, as shown below:

```
<script src="hello.js"></script>
```

This code snippet will find a file called "hello.js" and execute whatever JavaScript code is inside it. Make sure, however, that the JavaScript file is located in the same folder where the HTML file is kept.

### c. Instant JavaScript

If you'd like to test short JavaScript statements without having to modify the original source code, you can use the consoles provided by Google Chrome and Firefox by right clicking the webpage and clicking on "inspect element". In the console window/tab, you can type any JavaScript statement you want, and pressing enter executes it immediately. You can either choose this method to test the code snippets in this book, or if you'd like a more traditional approach, you can use the script tags for your JavaScript code and refresh your webpage to update the output. However, in the examples and exercises that'll be provided, the modern approach of using the console shall be used.

### Meet JavaScript

In order to give you a running start in JavaScript, you're going to try out a few lines of JavaScript code. For now, we're going to use the console to try out the commands (right-click any webpage, click inspect, and find the console tab). As you test the succeeding codes, make sure you don't just passively copy and paste them into the console. Observe the structure of the language and make a couple of guesses as to what the outputs would be before you check. This'll make it much easier for you to retain what you're learning.

Type your name and lock it in with two quotation marks, for example:

```
"Chris"
```

You've just created a string, which is basically just a collection of letters, numbers, and other symbols. We can do plenty of things even with a single string, but for now, let's make JavaScript count how many letters your name has:

```
"Chris".length
```

You should get 5. That being said, apart from dealing with strings, JavaScript also knows how to do math. Try adding the lengths of your first and last name, for example:

```
"Chris".length + "Nicholas".length
```

This would give you 13. Now go ahead and play around with this by using actual numbers and trying out multiplication (*), division (/), and subtraction(-).

Notice that while the commands you've put in so far are quite intuitive and easy to understand, programming languages require a lot more precision compared to human language. For instance, if you try to read the following "Tihs is a Coemplx Stenence," you'd be able to decipher the meaning, but in programming languages, if you so much as misplace a period, at best you'd receive an error - at worst a bug. For instance, try inputting the following code:

```
"Chris"l.ength
```

This would confuse the interpreter, even if you've simply misplaced the period.

Other than misspellings and misplaced symbols, another way to confuse the interpreter is to use commands it doesn't know about, for instance, if you type:

| bacon |
|---|

The interpreter would complain and say that 'bacon' is not defined. Because you've typed 'bacon' without the quotation marks, the interpreter thinks you're trying to make it perform the 'bacon' command, which doesn't exist in the JavaScript library as of now.

What if you simply want to type a bunch of hints and descriptions inside your code? You can tell the interpreter to ignore lines of code simply by typing '//' before the beginning of the line. For example:

| //This is a comment. The interpreter won't care about what I put here, even |
|---|
| //Valid commands like |
| //2+3 |
| //But by removing the '//', |
| 2+3 |
| //You should get 5. |

Now, you might be wondering why we're going through strings, mathematical operations, and comments with JavaScript when you've just wanted to make websites come to life, but before you can produce stunning animations, intelligent user-interaction, and other dynamic stuff, we have to lay the groundwork first. Now, let's have a little fun by creating your first pop-up dialogue box:

> confirm('Hi! You've just made your first pop-up dialogue. Congratulations! Click OK to go further!');

You after clicking OK, you should see a 'true' printed in the console. This is because JavaScript can also record user input, much like HTML. What's interesting with JavaScript, however, is that it doesn't need to refresh the page to ask for user input; it simply pops-up a small, separate window to ask you a question, and returns to the web page you were working on. This is especially useful when asking users for confirmation after they've filled up a form or decided to delete something - since no webpage refresh is required, the users can go back to whatever they're doing after clicking OK or CANCEL.

Okay, so far, you've managed to write your first string, ask JavaScript to compute its length, perform mathematical operations, write comments, and create pop-up confirmation dialogues. In order to make a website do really cool things, however, it needs to be able to get more than just a 'true' or a 'false' from a user, otherwise strings and mathematical computations would really be useless.

With this in mind, let's try making JavaScript ask for your name:

```
prompt('Hello! What's your name?');
```

After inputting your name, you should see whatever you've typed in the console output. Way to go!

## Storing Information

Every programming language needs to be able to store information; otherwise there's no way for it to make calculations and other important procedures, which is what computers were built for in the first place.

So far we've only been able to ask for the user's name, without even doing anything with it. This is because your name wasn't stored; it was just printed in the console. Let's use the power of variables so it can greet you after it asks for your name. Here's how:

```
var name = prompt('What's your name?');
alert('Hi, ' + name + '! It's nice to meet you.');
```

Now your program becomes more personal and more human, simply by responding to the user. Don't worry too much about the syntax if it overwhelms you; you'll learn more about what the alert() and prompt() functions do, and how you can make your own functions as we dive deeper into JavaScript.

## Conclusion

Congratulations! You've just gotten your first taste of JavaScript! It'll get even more interesting in the next chapter as we talk about what types of information you can use and what we can do with them. You'll also get your first glimpse into how you can help your program make decisions, as well as what to do if the your program doesn't behave the way you expect it to. It'll be quite a handful of information to take in one sitting, so take a break and come back when you're ready to dive further into the essentials of JavaScript.

# Chapter 3: JavaScript Essentials

Since this chapter is quite dense, here's an overview of what you can expect to learn:

1. Data types - how JavaScript classifies information. This is important because knowing what type of information you have will also tell you what you can do with that information (e.g., you can't multiply 5 with apples.)

2. Comparison Operators - lets you compare certain types of information (e.g., is 5 less than 10?). This is useful when you want to give the computer instructions that relies on certain conditions being met (e.g., allow the user to register only if the age is more than or equal to 18)

3. Console.log() - lets you display the output of a single line of code - useful when you want to see how information flows in your program per line of code.

4. Flow Control - if-else statements give the computer different instructions to execute depending on which condition is met (e.g., allow the user to enter site if the age is more than 18, otherwise, display an error message)

5. Debugging - when your program behaves erratically (e.g., misspelling the user's name or forgetting it completely), then you need to find which part of your code is messing up your program's behavior - this process is called

debugging. This can become rather daunting when the code spans more than a thousand lines - knowing where to look will come in handy.

So far, you've played with strings and numbers using JavaScript. In the programming world, these categories of information are referred to as data types.

## Data Types

Data types simply tell the computer how your information should be read. For instance, if you type the following into the console:

```
"5" + "5"
```

You'd get "55." This is because by enclosing 5 using quotation marks, you're telling the interpreter that you want 5 to be treated as a string, not a number. The addition operator, then, instead of adding the two numbers, combines the two strings. Now try removing the quotation marks and notice how the output changes to 10. There are different things you can do with different data types, so it's extremely important to know which one to use:

1. Strings - Anything you enclose in quotation marks will end up being a string. This can be a combination of letters, spaces, numbers, punctuation marks, and other symbols. Without strings, you wouldn't be able to get the user's name, address, email, and other important details.

2. Numbers - Self-explanatory; numbers are the ones you can perform addition, subtraction, multiplication, and division to, among other mathematical operations. Remember not to put quotation marks or you'll turn them into strings!

So far, we now have strings and numbers at our disposal, but remember the console output when you've tried playing with confirmation dialogues? Whenever you press OK, the console returns true, and whenever you press CANCEL, the console returns false. These outputs aren't surrounded by quotation marks, but they surely aren't numbers, so what in the world are they?

3. Booleans - booleans are data types that can only be either true or false. This is different from a string or a number, because it helps the computer make decisions based on whether or not certain conditions are met. For example, if you want to prevent minors from registering in your site, you'd have to have some sort of code to separate minors from the adults, like:

```
var age = 17
age >= 18
```

The console, then, returns false because the age is under 18. Now try the following mathematical expressions out and see what you get:

```
5 > 10
```

> 6 < 12

The first line should return false, while the second line should return true.

## Comparison Operators

So far, we've talked about three data types (numbers, strings, and booleans), as well as some basic mathematical operators (+, -, *, /). What you've just used to test out booleans, however, are comparison operators (<, >, =), which are extremely important in managing the flow of your program. Here's the complete list and what they can do:

> Greater than

< Less than

>= Greater than or equal to

<= Less than or equal to

== Equal to

!= Not equal to

To test out these operators, replace the '@' symbol with the correct operator in the following statements in order to make the console output true:

> console.log(5 @ 1);

```
console.log(1 @ 5);

console.log(5 @ 2);

console.log(1 @ 6);

console.log(5 @ 5);

console.log(10 @ 5);
```

## Knowing what the Interpreter is Thinking

Notice how the JavaScript interpreter only gives you the latest output of the commands you type in, so if you've typed in three lines of code that should have different outputs:

```
5 > 10

6 < 12

7 > 14
```

Executing them all at the same time in the console, you'd only get the result of the last line (false).

You can, instead, enter each line of code individually so you can see the output of each command, but this gets especially tedious in larger bits of code. When you get to more complicated stuff, you'll eventually run into more errors and bugs. When this happens, you'll want to know what happens in specific commands you give so that you can pinpoint exactly where things go wrong.

console.log() takes whatever code you put inside and logs its execution to the console. That being said, let's see console.log() in action:

```
console.log(5 > 10)

console.log(6 < 12)

console.log(7 > 14)
```

Now you can see the output of each line of code!

## Flow Control

You now know the most basic data types, mathematical operators, comparison operators, and a couple of neat console tricks. In order to make them useful, however, we need to be able to manipulate the flow of commands. For instance, if you wanted to create a user registration form that asks for the user's name, email address, age, and password, you'd first declare the variables as:

```
var name;

var email;

var age;

var password;
```

Now we'd need to store the user's input. For now, we use the prompt function:

```
name = prompt('What's your name?');

email = prompt('What's your email?');

age = prompt('What's your age?');

password = prompt('Please enter your desired password: ');
```

Assuming you've entered the right kind of information in the data fields, the name, email, age, and password variables now have the right type of data to process and store. What if, however, the user leaves the email field blank, or the age field with a letter? We can't just let the program continue if some of the vital fields of information don't have the right kind of data, therefore we use flow control statements. The first one we shall discuss is the if statement.

## If Statement

If you've already programmed before, the structure of an if statement in JavaScript should be almost identical to the one you're familiar with:

```
if (<condition>)
{
    <action>
}
```

If you haven't already programmed before, an if-statement basically tells the computer to do whatever is inside the curly brackets ({}) if the if condition is true. If we want to, for instance, prevent the user from entering a blank field, we can do the following:

```
name = prompt('What's your name?');
if (name.length == 0)
{
    name = prompt('You cannot leave this empty. What's your name?');
}
```

```
email = prompt('What's your email?');

if (email.length == 0)

{

    email = prompt('You cannot leave this empty. What's your email address?');

}


age = prompt('What's your age?');

if (age.length == 0)

{

    age = prompt('You cannot leave this empty. What's your age?');

}


password = prompt('Please enter your desired password: ');

if (password.length == 0)

{

    password = prompt('You cannot leave this empty. Please enter your desired password:');
```

```
}
```

The code can seem overwhelming for the first-time programmer, but when you read each line carefully, you'll see that they follow quite a neat and logical structure:

1) First, since the prompt() function gives you whatever the user types in, you store the string inside a variable so you can use it later in the program.

2) The if statements check if the variable is empty by checking if the length is equal to zero or not.

   a) If the length is equal to zero, it asks for input again.

   b) If the length isn't equal to zero, it doesn't ask for input again.

Take note that this sample code only serves to illustrate how the if statement works. Under no circumstances should you keep using the prompt() function to ask the user for information.

Now, what if you want to do something else in case your first condition isn't met? For instance, what if you want to say "Your name is <name>. Got it!" after the user types in a valid name? Then we add an else condition, followed by a second pair of curly braces that enclose the second set of commands:

```
name = prompt('What's your name?');

if (name.length == 0)
```

```
{
    name = prompt('You cannot leave this empty. What's your name?');
}
else
{
    alert('Your name is ' + name + '. Got it!');
}


email = prompt('What's your email?');
if (email.length == 0)
{
    email = prompt('You cannot leave this empty. What's your email address?');
}
else
{
    alert('Your email is ' + email + '. Got it!');
}
```

```
age = prompt('What's your age?');

if (age.length == 0)

{

    age = prompt('You cannot leave this empty. What's your age?');

}

else

{

    alert('Your age is ' + age + '. Got it!');

}


password = prompt('Please enter your desired password: ');

if (password.length == 0)

{

    password = prompt('You cannot leave this empty. Please enter your desired password:');

}

else

{
```

```
    alert('Your password is ' + password + '. Got it!');
}
```

Now your code sounds a little more human, as it responds better to user input. Try messing around with the code and see how the interpreter changes the output depending on the conditions met with the if-else statements.

## Debugging

So far, you've managed to play around with variables, data types, mathematical operators, comparison operators, user prompts, confirmation dialogues, and alerts, and lastly, if-else statements. Don't worry if you make a couple of mistakes; computers are intrinsically literal and will not tolerate the tiniest syntactical mistakes. That being said, here are a couple of codes that don't seem to work as intended. Change the following code snippets so that you can produce the appropriate output!

```
var name = "Chris";
alert('Hi ' + 'name' + '! It's nice to meet you.');
```

In this code snippet, the output is supposed to be "Hi Chris! It's nice to meet you." What's the current output and what do you think is wrong with the code? Notice that the console doesn't complain and throw you an error message when you execute this code. This kind of problem is called a 'bug,' because while the

JavaScript interpreter sees nothing wrong with this code, it doesn't work as the creator intended.

Now try to correct this code snippet that contains both bugs and errors:

```
var name;

var age;


name = prompt('What's your name?');

if (name.length = 0);

{

   name = prompt('You cannot leave this empty. What's your name?');

}

else (name.length != 0)

{

   alert('Your name is ' + name + '. Got it!');

}


age = prompt('What's your age?');

if (age.length = 0)
```

```
{
    age = prompt('You cannot leave this empty. What's your age?');
}
else (name.length != 0)
{
    alert('Your age is ' + age + '. Got it!');
}
```

This code is a distorted version of a previous sample code, so you may try to compare the codes and see why this one doesn't work. If you feel stuck, you can check out a program called 'linter,' which is a handy tool that checks your code for errors and tells you which lines have them. It's good exercise to practice your debugging skills now, because when you create more complex programs, debugging becomes almost routine.

**What to look for when debugging:**

Looking for bugs and errors can be quite overwhelming if you don't know where to look. Here are some of the most common mistakes programmers make when coding:

1. Using '=' instead of '==' to compare two values - the '=' sign in programming is used as an assignment operator, which means that if you use this instead of the '==' sign, you end up replacing the value of the variable on the left hand side of the equation with the value on the right hand side of the equation.

2. Misplacing the semicolon - just as periods end sentences in the English language, semicolons end statements in JavaScript, as well as other programming languages like C, Java, etc. If, for instance, you've accidentally put a semicolon in the middle of a statement, JavaScript would see the statement as incomplete and produce an error for it.

3. Misusing the quotation marks - quotation marks tell the interpreter that you're using a string, so if you enclose a variable or a number in quotation marks, you're effectively turning them into strings. This'll lead to anomalies when you try to perform numerical operations onto numbers that you've accidentally enclosed in quotation marks.

4. Misspelling functions - as I've mentioned before, computers are precise, sometimes to a fault; it can't understand anything you misspell. Fortunately, if you misspell a function or a statement, the interpreter will

throw you an error telling you that the expression you're using is undefined.

So far, these are only the most common mistakes newbies tend to make, but along the way you should be able to see bugs and errors quite easily as you get more practice making more complex codes.

**Recap**

We've covered quite a lot of concepts so far, so let's review what we've learned:

1. Variables and data types

    - numbers - can be integers or numbers that contain decimals (e.g., 3.14, 5, 100)

    - strings - anything you enclose in quotation marks (e.g., "5", "I am a JavaScript master", "I love the number 7")

    - booleans - true or false

In order to declare a variable, simply type:

```
var <variable name> = <value>;
```

You can also just declare the variable name without the value if you don't have one yet:

```
var <variable name>;
```

JavaScript doesn't care what type of data you put in. If you've programmed in C or Java, you might have been used to declaring the variable's data type (int, float, char, etc.), but in JavaScript, you can put anything in a variable without any problems.

2. Pop-up boxes

    - alert("Hi There!") - you can pop-up alerts to the user.

    - confirm("Are you sure?") - you can ask for a confirmation from the user.

    - prompt("Type anything here.") - you can ask for input from the user

3. Flow-control

    - if-else statement - in a nutshell, if the first condition is met, then do whatever's in the first bracket enclosure and skip the 'else' part. Otherwise, go to the bracket enclosure for the 'else' condition and do whatever's inside it.

Congratulations! You've gone through a lot of programming basics through JavaScript! If you've come this far, then you should be able to finish the next few chapters in flying colors. In the next chapter, we'll get into the nitty-gritty details of mathematical operations and substrings. Take a break, and if you're ready to go deeper, go ahead and proceed to Chapter 4.

# Chapter 4: Functions and Data Manipulation

Being another dense chapter, here's a quick overview of the things you can expect to learn:

1. Mathematical Precedence - learning about mathematical precedence helps you make sure that the mathematical operations, no matter how complex, are carried out in the correct order (e.g., 5*(5+2) gives you a different output compared to 5*5+2)

2. Modulo Operator - this operator gives you the remainder of a number divided by another number. This operation is used often enough to warrant having its own operator symbol (%)

3. String Manipulation - there are times when you don't need to use the whole string in your code, such as when you want to display previews of text that span hundreds of lines if displayed completely.

4. Functions - functions allow you to repeat a huge set of instructions that could span hundreds or thousands of lines simply by invoking the function name!

5. Optimization - everyone prefers shorter code; it takes up much less space, and it's also easier to debug. The trick, however, is finding the balance between how readable a code can be through elaboration, and how short and

concise a code can be through a couple of syntactic 'shortcuts'.

6. Global and Local Variables - some variables live only inside the function and don't exist outside it - these are local variables. Variables that live throughout the whole code are called global variables.

## Mathematical Precedence

So far, you've dealt with basic mathematical operators and performed only single operations. In programming, however, one rarely makes programs that have only one mathematical operation per line. For instance, if your site wants to find out how old the user is in terms of minutes, you'd have to do something like:

---
var age = prompt('How old are you?');

alert('You are ' + age*365*24*60 + ' minutes old');

---

With that in mind, you have to make sure that the operations are done in the correct order. To do this, you'll have to remember the following rules of precedence:

1. ( ) - anything you enclose in parenthesis will be done first

2. \* and / - multiplication and division are done first before addition and subtraction

3. + and - - addition and subtraction are done last.

Here are a couple of exercises to help you visualise mathematical precedence:

```
5 * 10 + 3 - 5 / 20
```

This would produce 52.75 because the multiplication and division symbol takes precedence over the subtraction symbol. The story changes when you add parenthesis to the procedure:

```
5 * 10 + (3 - 5) / 20
```

Notice how the result now becomes 49.9 because the parenthesis gave whatever operation is inside it precedence over other operations. Here's another example:

```
(5 * 10 + 3 - 5) / 20
```

Now the answer becomes 2.4, as everything inside the parenthesis is done first before it's divided by 20. Inside the parenthesis, the usual rules of precedence apply, so if you want a lower-precedence operation to happen first, you'll need to enclose it in another set of parenthesis.

## A new contender: modulo

In basic math class, there were only four mathematical operators. In programming, however, there's an interesting fifth operator called *modulo (%)*. When placed between two numbers, it divides them and gives you the remainder. Remember that programming requires conciseness and precision; it has no room for extraneous symbols and features, which means that there's a good reason why the modulo operator exists. One interesting application of the modulo operator is testing whether a number is even or odd:

```
var num = prompt('Give me a number: ');
if (num % 2 != 0)
{
   alert('The number is odd.');
}
else
{
   alert('The number is even.');
}
```

Pitfall alert:

One common mistake novice programmers make when trying to test whether a number is even or odd is to check if the remainder of two numbers is equal to 1. At a glance, this might seem logical, as for every POSITIVE number you divide by two, the remainder can only be one or zero (e.g., 13 % 2 = 1, and 12 % 2 = 0). A problem arises, however, when you input a negative number; since the remainder is no longer equal to positive 1, then the program starts to act erratically. These kinds of mistakes are quite easy to make, so whenever you try out solutions to a problem, make sure to test the code thoroughly with a wide range of input (in this example, the user would've discovered the pitfall quite easily if he were to test negative numbers).

Now, try modifying the following code so that it displays "Greetings from planet JavaScript!"

```
if (14 % 2 != 0)

{

   console.log("Greetings");

}

if (15 % 2 != 0)

{

   console.log("to");

}

if (10 % 2 != 0)

{
```

```
    console.log("from");
}
if (9 % 2 != 0)
{
    console.log("atmosphere");
}
if (5 % 3 != 0)
{
    console.log("planet");
}
if (20 % 2 != 0)
{
    console.log("JavaScript");
}
```

# Messing with strings

So far, we've managed to play around with numbers, from performing regular mathematical operations, to comparing values, to seeing what the modulo operator can do. Now, we're going to mess around with strings and see what you can do with them.

The first thing we're going to do is to explore substrings, which are basically just parts of a whole string. Substrings were created because sometimes, people just need a small preview of a whole text. For instance, when you search for anything online, the results page gives you only the first few words from the content of the sites listed, allowing you to skim through multiple sites quickly and efficiently. The keyword here is 'preview' - you don't want to overwhelm users with information, so if you have large sets of information, you're most likely going to need substrings.

Here's how the code works:

```
"I am a sentence".substring(2, 7)
```

The output should be "am a ". As an exercise, try changing the numbers inside the parenthesis and see which letters you get.

The function, substring() requires two numbers - one to tell the interpreter where to start cutting the string and one to tell the interpreter where to stop. In programming, however, we always start with the number 0, which is why if you want to cut-off only the last few parts of a string, you'd need to do something like:

```
"I am a sentence".substring(0, 7)
```

The output should now be "I am a ".

If, on the other hand, you'd like to cut-off only the first few parts of a string, you can try something like:

```
var sentence = "I am a sentence";

sentence.substring(4, sentence.length)
```

The reason why we use sentence.length instead of manually inputting 15 (the length of the sentence variable) is because in programming, we want to make sure that tiny changes in code won't break a program. Imagine if we've used a fixed length to get the last few characters of a variable that gets updated every now and then, for instance:

```
sentence = "I am now a longer sentence and I can stretch as far as I can";

sentence.substring(4, 15)
```

This'd give you a different output, and depending on how your webpage works, this might wreak havoc on your data. That being said, always be careful with the parameters of the substring function!

Now that you have more tools at your disposal when dealing with strings and numbers, we can now proceed to what we can consider the pinnacle of modularity in the world of programming: functions.

## Functions

Functions let you build a program almost like a robot - with every part serving a specific purpose, like hands for grasping objects and feet for walking or running. Apart from this, the concept of functions is also founded on a philosophy that every programmer will eventually learn and live by: ruthless simplicity and minimalism in coding.

In programming, people always want to find ways to make the computer do more while typing fewer lines of code. Functions allow programmers to repeat a set of instructions without having to retype the same set of lines. Its analogue to real life would be like teaching someone how to bake a cake - at first, you give them precise instructions, like how to preheat the oven, how to mix the ingredients, etc. In the future, however, you should no longer need to give a new set of instructions; while different cakes may need different ingredients, the general instructions are almost always the same. No baker wants to be told again and again how to bake a cake; once they're taught how to bake a cake, you'd only have to give them a list of ingredients and the cake you want, and the cook would know what to do. Functions are like that; you only have to create them once, and you can call them again in your code in case you need to do the same set of instructions, but with different input and output.

Here's what a function looks like:

```
var computeSum = function (firstNumber, secondNumber)
{
  var result = firstNumber + secondNumber;
  console.log(result);
};
```

In the first line, you declare the name of the function (in this example, it's computeSum), and the data you want to pass inside it (in this example, we have firstNumber and secondNumber).

Inside the function, enclosed by brackets ({ }), you see two lines that first add the two variables indicated in the first line, and then log the result to the console.

Going back to our example of baking, the code inside the brackets would be the precise set of instructions that you only give once, and the function name is what you invoke whenever you need to tell the baker to bake a new cake, together with the ingredients. It'd look roughly like this when you put it into code:

```
var bakeCake = function (ingredient1, ingredient2, ingredient3)
{
  var ovenTemperature = 300;
  var mixedIngredients = ingredient1 + ingredient2 + ingredient3;
```

```
    var finishedCake = mixedIngredients * ovenTemperature;

    alert('Finished making a delicious cake with ' + ingredient1 + ', '
+ ingredient2 + ', ' + ingredient3 + '!');

    console.log(finishedCake);

};
```

Whenever you need to bake a cake, then, you'd only need to type this:

```
bakeCake('eggs', 'chocolate', 'flour')
```

This becomes really handy should you find yourself having to type the same chunk of code. Not only does your code look much neater, but it also makes debugging much easier; when a part of your site doesn't work, you only need to find the function responsible for the bug instead of checking your whole code line-by-line.

In a nutshell, a function takes in a bunch of information, does something with the information, and then gives you something out of that. Here's a step-by-step guide on how to create a function:

1. Declare a function using var, and give it a name just as you would to any data type. Programmers have agreed to a naming convention wherein the name should always start with a lowercase letter and then uppercase for each

succeeding word that follows. This is called the *lower camel case convention* (e.g., anExampleOfTheCamelCaseConvention).

2. After giving the name of the function, you use the word 'function' to tell the interpreter that you're making a function, not a string, number, or boolean.

3. Inside the parenthesis that comes after 'function' are your *function parameters*. As you may have noticed from our bakeCake function, ingredient1, ingredient2, and ingredient3 were replaced by eggs, chocolate, and flour. You can think of the former as variable names, and the latter as the values inside the variables, such that by invoking 'bakeCake('eggs', 'chocolate', 'flour'),' you're effectively assigning 'eggs' to ingredient1; 'chocolate' to ingredient2; and 'flour' to ingredient3.

4. Inside the brackets would be your function body. This is the place where you do stuff to the parameters you've asked for (ingredient1, ingredient2, and ingredient3 for this example).

Take note that every line of code inside the brackets should end with a semicolon. At the end of the function, just after the closing bracket, you'll also need a semicolon to tell the computer that you're done creating the function.

## Return Values

So far, the functions are almost standalone, in a sense that all they do is execute a whole bunch of statements. What's interesting about them, however, is that we can also use functions the same way we use numbers, strings, and booleans when we add a return value. A return value is any type of data given back by a function. Whenever a return statement is invoked, the computer typically assumes that the function is done doing what it needs to do and therefore throws whatever is in the return statement back to the code that called the function. For instance, going back to our computeSum() function:

---

var computeSum = function (firstNumber, secondNumber)

{

  var result = firstNumber + secondNumber;

  console.log(result);

};

---

Try accessing the 'result' variable outside the function call by moving the console.log(result) command just outside the computeSum() function. You should encounter an error saying that the variable 'result' is not defined. In programming, when you declare variables inside a function, they only exist inside that function. If you want to get the result, you'll have to set it as the return value:

55

```
var computeSum = function (firstNumber, secondNumber)
{
    var result = firstNumber + secondNumber;
    return result;
};
```

With this, you can now treat the computeSum() function like a number! Try these codes out for yourself:

```
console.log(computeSum(5, 5) + 10)
console.log(computeSum(7, 8) / 10)
console.log(computeSum(9, 10) - 10)
console.log(computeSum(4, 4) * 10)
console.log(computeSum(42, 34) % 2)
```

## Optimisation: Finding the Perfect Balance Between Readability and Conciseness

Now that you're learning more and more complex ways to code, now is the perfect time to discuss code readability. One easy way to spot a novice programmer is by looking at how long and how readable the code is. For instance, our computeSum() function, while perfectly readable, could still be shortened to:

```
var computeSum = function (firstNumber, secondNumber)
{
   return firstNumber + secondNumber;
};
```

This shortens the code by one line without looking messy. There are times, however, when you have to choose carefully whether choosing to be concise can make your code too difficult to understand, for instance, take a look at this simple if-else statement:

```
if (5 > 7)
{
   console.log('5 is greater than 7');
}
else
```

```
{
    console.log('7 is greater than 5');
}
```

It's easy enough to read, but you can actually reduce this to a single line using what's called a *ternary expression*:

```
5 > 7 ? console.log('5 is greater than 7') : console.log('7 is greater than 5');
```

The statement becomes much more compact now, but it reduces readability as well. The ternary expression should really only be used when you're assigning a value conditionally, e.g.,

```
var greaterNum = 5 > 7 ? 5 : 7;
```

This line assigns 5 to greaterNum if it is greater than 7, otherwise it assigns 7 to greaterNum.

That being said, remember that there are many ways to make your code more compact and easy to read. For compactness, you need to make sure that your optimisations are well-warranted and used correctly (as in the case of the ternary operator). As for being easy-to-read, it really has a lot to do with using the right names for your variables and functions, as well as being consistent with the way you type your code.

## Global and Local Variables

We've talked about variables not being accessible anywhere else in your code except within the functions they were created in. These are called local variables. Global variables are the ones declared outside functions and can be accessible anywhere within your code. For example:

```
var x = 10; // this is a global variable because it isn't declared inside the function


var turnToZero = function(number) {
    number = 0;
    console.log("The value of x is now: " + x);
};


turnToZero(x);


console.log("Outside the function the value of x is: " + x);
```

Notice how the variable 'x' can still be accessed inside the turnToZero() function. Here's where a lot of beginners get confused: when you pass a variable to a function, just like what we did when we invoked:

```
turnToZero(x);
```

You're just copying the value of x into the function, and placing it into the temporary variable named 'number'. This means that when you do stuff to the variable 'number', you're not really doing anything to x. This is why the turnToZero function is useless; when you pass a variable into it, only the value of the temporary variable is changed, not the actual variable.

That being said, you don't have to pass a global variable to a function in order to modify its value. We can simply do the following:

```
var x = 10; // this is a global variable because it isn't declared inside the function

var turnToZero = function() {
    x = 0;
    console.log("The value of x is now: " + x);
};
console.log("Before calling the function, the value of x is: " + x);

turnToZero();
```

> console.log("After calling the function, the value of x is now: " + x);

In a nutshell, the var keyword, apart from telling the computer that you're declaring a variable, also tells the interpreter to create a new variable in the current scope, which is why if it's created inside a function, it'll only exist inside a function, and if it's created outside a function, it'll exist throughout the whole code. With this in mind, you might be wondering why one would even need local variables if global variables are much easier to use. The reason for this is that global variables can make it harder to read and debug programs. You'll notice this when you start creating more complex JavaScript codes, but for now, it's best not to try modifying global variables inside a function unless you know exactly why you're doing it.

## Conclusion

With a better knowledge of functions, variables, and data manipulation, you can now create cleaner, more efficient code! In the next chapter, you'll learn about how you can store different types of information under one variable name (arrays), as well as how you can repeatedly run statements for a certain number of times (loops). Take note that while loops and arrays aren't really that complicated to learn and use, it's important to remain meticulous when you code so you don't end up crashing your browser. That being said, feel free to take a short break before you get into Chapter 5.

# Chapter 5: Loops and Arrays

We've talked about functions and how they're made so that we don't need togive the same set of instructions again and again. Now, what if you want to, say, print a hundred lines of "I will not waste precious console space" on the console? You can do the following:

```
console.log("I will not waste precious console space");

console.log("I will not waste precious console space");

console.log("I will not waste precious console space");

//... assume that there are 96 more of the console message here

console.log("I will not waste precious console space");
```

Since functions serve to make our codes cleaner, we can opt to do this instead:

```
var consoleMessage = function()
{
   console.log("I will not waste precious console space");

   console.log("I will not waste precious console space");

   console.log("I will not waste precious console space");
```

```
    //... assume that there are 96 more of the console message here
    console.log("I will not waste precious console space");
};
```

so that when you can just invoke the consoleMessage() function to perform the hundred-line command. Unfortunately, it's still rather unwieldy to print so many redundant lines of code. Since we always want to shorten the code we write whenever possible, we opt for a more efficient way to repeat lines of code by using for-loops!

## For-Loops

For loops tell the computer to do a bunch of stuff for a specified number of times. The format of the for loop is:

```
for (var <variable name> = <initial value>; <condition>; <iteration>)
{
    <action to be repeated>
}
```

Here's what it'd look like if we were to adapt the previous example to use the for-loop:

```
for (var counter = 1; counter <= 100; counter++)
{
    console.log("I will not waste precious console space");
}
```

Instead of manually typing the console.log statement a hundred times, we can use a for loop to do it for us. Now, let's take a closer look at the parts of a for loop:

```
var counter = 1
```

This is the first part of the for loop. We're only creating this variable in order to keep track of the number of times the chunk of code inside the for-loop has been executed. When the for-loop ends, this variable vanishes.

```
counter <= 100
```

This is the condition that needs to be fulfilled in order for the code inside the for-loop to be executed. As long as this statement is true, the code inside the for-loop will be repeated again and again. Take care not to create a condition that's always true (e.g., 100 == 100) or else you'll have what's known as an infinite loop!

```
counter++
```

This is an iteration statement that adds 1 to the variable 'counter'. This makes sure that eventually, the counter will reach 100 and will therefore cause the 'counter <= 100' statement to return false. Without this statement, the counter will stay at 1, and the 'counter <= 100' statement will always return true!

These three statements are what help for-loops run a chunk of code for a precise number of times. Here are a bunch of additional tips to help you create for-loops better:

1. You can also count backwards if you want, changing the condition from (<) or (<=) to (>) or( >=), and then decrementing (counter--).

2. You can also increment or decrement with any other number by writing something like "counter+=n" or "counter-=n"where n is the number you want to add or subtract to the counter.

3. Be careful with the conditions you set! If you create a for-loop that results in an infinite loop, your browser will crash!

That being said, here's a code that'll result in an infinite loop, and consequently, a browser crash:

```
for (var counter = 1; counter <= 10; counter--)
{
    console.log(counter);
```

```
}
```

As an exercise, change this for-loop so that it ends up displaying the numbers 1-10 in the console.

**Arrays**

If you wanted to, say, record ten names, without using arrays, you'd have to do something like:

```
var name1, name2, name3, name4, name5, name6, name7, name8, name9, name10;
```

And this is only for declaring the variables! Here's how messy it would be if you actually have to store user input using this method:

```
for (var counter = 1; counter <= 10; counter++)
{
   if(counter == 1)
   {
      name1 = prompt('Please enter name 1: ');
   }
   if(counter == 2)
```

```
{
    name2 = prompt('Please enter name 2: ');
}
if(counter == 3)
{
    name3 = prompt('Please enter name 3: ');
}
if(counter == 4)
{
    name4 = prompt('Please enter name 4: ');
}
if(counter == 5)
{
    name5 = prompt('Please enter name 5: ');
}
if(counter == 6)
{
    name6 = prompt('Please enter name 6: ');
}
```

```
if(counter == 7)

{

    name7 = prompt('Please enter name 7: ');

}

if(counter == 8)

{

    name8 = prompt('Please enter name 8: ');

}

if(counter == 9)

{

    name9 = prompt('Please enter name 9: ');

}

if(counter == 10)

{

    name10 = prompt('Please enter name 10: ');

}

}
```

Now imagine if social media sites used this method to register the users; programmers would have to keep recoding the site in order to accommodate more users! Fortunately, we have arrays to help us.

Arrays, in a nutshell, can store lists of data that could even have different data types. The data stored have fixed positions, so you're sure of where each data is placed and can therefore retrieve them reliably. Here are examples of array declarations:

---

var strings = ["apple","grapes","tomatoes"];

var numbers = [1, 2, 3, 4, 5];

var stringsAndNumbers = ["Oceans", 11];

---

As you may have noticed, the declaration statements for arrays are pretty similar to the declaration statements for regular variables; the only difference is that the data are enclosed in braces and separated by commas. If you want to create an empty array, you can leave the braces blank and add a couple of items later using the push() function, for instance:

---

var numbers = [];

for (var counter = 1; counter <= 10; counter++)

{

  numbers.push(counter);

}

---

Now we can go back to our previous attempt at getting ten names! Let's see how using arrays drastically improves our code:

```
var names = [];

for (var counter = 1; counter <= 10; counter++)

{

  names.push(prompt('Please enter name ' + counter + ':'));

  console.log('Obtained name ' + counter);

}
```

Our code just became much more efficient and much better to look at! Congratulations!

So far, you've learned how to declare arrays and put stuff in them, but how exactly can we access what's inside them? Well, the position of the items we place inside the array stay in the same spot, so we only need to know what the name of the array is and the numerical position of the item we've stored.

One small caveat though: in programming, we always start counting from 0, so if you have 10 items in an array, your first item will be in the 0th place while your last item will be in the 9th place. That being said, if you want to access the names you've just collected, simply do something like:

```
console.log(names[0]); //for the 1st name

console.log(names[9]); //for the 10th name
```

Sometimes, when you just keep adding stuff to an array, you may lose track of how big it is. Fortunately we can just use the '.length' keyword we normally add to strings in order to count the number of characters. For instance, if we were to count the number of names stored in our variable 'names', we'd need to just append .length to 'names:

```
names.length
```

Great job! You've now learned how to create arrays and how to put stuff inside them. As an exercise, create a for-loop that prints out every name from the 'names' array into the console. Hint: the 'counter' variable comes in handy when keeping track of the index of the array.

Notice how we're slowly building up your arsenal of programming tools:

1. Variables - allow you to store information so you could do interesting stuff with them later

2. Mathematical Operators - allow you to perform calculations

3. Comparison Operators - allow you to check how a value is greater, less than, equal, or not equal to another value.

4. if-else statements - allow you to give the computer a bunch of stuff to do depending on the circumstance

5. functions - allow you to keep your code clean and easy to manage

6. for-loops - allow you to make the computer do stuff for a specific number of times

7. arrays - allow you to store a list of information under one variable name

These are, at the most basic level, what programming is - giving precise instructions to computers in the most efficient manner possible.

## A Mini Project: Text-Searching

Now that you have a basic arsenal of programming tools, let's create a short program that tries to search for a string in a block of text.

```
var textBlock = "I can create a really really long sentence but never mind.";

var queryWord = "really";


var matchCount = 0;


//loops through each letter of the textBlock variable

for (var counter = 0; counter < textBlock.length; counter++)
{
   //The first condition checks if the first letter of the query word is in the current index of the textBlock; this would mean that we might get a match.

   //The second condition checks if the remaining text from the textBlock left unchecked is at least bigger than the queryWord (You can't exactly look for the word, "Apple" from "Ap").


   if((textBlock[counter] == queryWord[0]) && (textBlock.length-counter >= queryWord.length))
```

```
{
    var match = true;
    for(var counter1 = 0; counter1 < queryWord.length; counter1++)
    {
        if(!(textBlock[counter+counter1] == queryWord[counter1]))
        {
            match = false;
            break;
        }
    }
    if(match==true)
    {
        matchCount++;
    }
  }
}
```

```
console.log('Done! Total matches: ' + matchCount);
```

Whew! That was quite a lot of for-loops and if-statements, wasn't it? If the code seems rather intimidating to you, don't worry; we'll take you through it step-by-step. First, let's go over what a lot of tutorials gloss over when explaining how these programs work: how can you explain the concept of looking for a word in a block of text to a computer that only knows how to perform precise instructions? We'd have to convert the problem, then, from the english form, "I want to find a word in a block of text" into a more specific set of commands. Here's a set of thinking points to consider:

- Blocks of text and words are strings; you can access each letter using the string's index.

- You can compare letters to see if they're equal, e.g., 'E'=='B' returns false, and 'A'=='A' returns true.

The trick is to break the process down further into simpler procedures. For instance, here is a sample block of text:

```
var numberSet = "One two three four five";
var queryString = "two";
```

While looking for a string is easy enough for humans, for computers, it's a little more complicated. In this example, we are to locate 'two', which one easily sees but the computer doesn't, therefore we have to start looking from the beginning of the string to the end. The letter enclosed in brackets is the one we're currently comparing:

"[O]ne two three four five" vs. "[t]wo"

In code for, that'd be:

```
numberSet[0] == queryString[0];
```

As you've noticed, we don't immediately compare the two words; we get their first letter and check if they're equal. Since in this first scenario, "O" isn't equal to "t", we move on to the next letter:

"O[n]e two three four five" vs. "[t]wo"

which in code, would translate to:

```
numberSet[1] == queryString[0];
```

again, this returns false, so we move on until we get to a match:

"One [t]wo three four five" vs. "[t]wo"

which translates to:

```
numberSet[4] == queryString[0];
```

Now, we can't yet make the assumption that we've found "two" in the numberSet; we've only gotten a match for the first letter. It's still possible that we're just coming across a number that also starts with 't', e.g., three, thirty, etc. That being said, we'd have to then compare the second letter of "two" to the next letter in the numberSet:

"One t[w]o three four five" vs. "t[w]o"

which translates to:

numberSet[5] == queryString[1];

The statement remains true, and if you try checking the next letter, it'd also return true. Since the statement continues to be true until the last letter of "two", then we can now say that we've found 1 instance of "two" in the numberSet. The search, however, still has to continue until the last three letters of the numberSet:

"One two three four f[i]ve" vs. "[t]wo"

which translates to:

numberSet[20] == queryString[0];

Since this statement will return false, there's no need to go further to 'v' or 'e' since the remaining letters are too small to provide a match for "two".

**Still Confused?**

If you find yourself confused and overwhelmed with the process of converting problems from English to JavaScript, it's a good idea to come up with a list of how you want your program to handle the problem. For instance, here's the procedure list for our string-search program:

3) Run through the letters of the block of text

    a) Does the current letter match the first letter of our query string?

        i) If yes, run through the rest of the letters of our query string and compare each letter to the succeeding letter of the block of text.

        ii) If no, proceed to next letter.

    b) Was there a match?

        i) If yes, record it

        ii) If no, continue

Of course, there are plenty of optimizations that you may discover in the future that'll make this program use less resources, but for now, this is a great example of how one needs to learn the art of reverse-engineering. As you start creating more and more complex JavaScript applications, you learn more about how you can efficiently translate human problems into computer-understandable problems.

## Conclusion

Congratulations! You've just learned about for-loops, arrays, and how everything else you've learned so far comes together to help you write useful programs! As you've noticed in our latest example, programming entails more than just learning the syntax of a language. In the same way that poetry requires not only a certain level of mastery of the language, but also a certain level of mastery in self-expression, programming requires a certain level of mastery in breaking down problems, as well as coming up with working solutions to them. The language simply serves to provide a concrete structure for your solution. In the next chapter, we'll add some improvements to our current program, as well as add a couple of flow control techniques to your arsenal. So far you've taken in quite a handful of information, so feel free to take a break and come back when you're ready.

# Chapter 6: Mastering Flow Control

So far, we've taken up if-else statements and for-loops. While you can make fast and efficient programs using only these two, there are more tools that can help you fine-tune your programs. In this chapter, we'll learn about these new tools, as well as optimization techniques to wrap-up the procedural part of JavaScript (JavaScript is a dynamic language, so it can be procedural, object-oriented, etc. depending on how you use it).

**While Loops**

The first kind of loop you've used in this book is the for-loop, which uses three parameters:

1. Initial value of the counter

2. Condition for the loop to repeat

3. Iteration of the counter

What if, however, you need to repeat something based on a non-numerical condition? For instance, what if, say, going back to our lesson on if-statements back in Chapter 3, we've talked about repeating the request for user input if the user doesn't enter anything. The if-statements, however, only lets you do this once. For-loops, while useful in repeating commands for a specific number of times, it doesn't fit particularly well in this dilemma since you want to keep asking the user for input until he puts in something valid; you can't realistically predict how many times the user will leave something blank.

That being said, when we can't easily tell when we need to stop looping at the start of the code, we can use a while loop. Here's what it looks like:

```
while(<condition>)
{
    <action>
    <something that should eventually make the condition false>
}
```

Basically, the while loop is just a for-loop without the counter and its iteration. The good and bad thing about this is that you can put just about any condition that returns true or false, and inside the brackets, you can put any statement that eventually turns the condition false. For instance:

```
var keepLooping = true;
while (keepLooping)
{
    console.log("Just keep looping!");
    keepLooping = false;
```

```
}
```

Notice that we've executed the code only once because we've set keepLooping to false. You can also use while loops to do the same thing for-loops do, for instance:

```
var counter = 0;
while(counter <= 10)
{
    console.log(counter);
    counter++;
}
```

The equivalent of this for the for-loop is:

```
for(var counter = 0; counter <= 10; counter++)
{
    console.log(counter);
}
```

But as you see, the for-loop does this much more cleanly than the while loop, especially since the variable 'counter' only exists inside the for-loop and is cleaned up when the loop ends. As for the while loop, the counter keeps its value as long as the program remains running.

Now let's use while loops to optimize our code back in Chapter 3:

```
var name = prompt('What's your name?');

while (name.length == 0)

{

   name = prompt('You cannot leave this empty. What's your name?');

}


alert('Your name is ' + name + '. Got it!');


var email = prompt('What's your email?');

while (email.length == 0)

{

   email = prompt('You cannot leave this empty. What's your email address?');

}
```

83

```
alert('Your email is ' + email + '. Got it!');


var age = prompt('What's your age?');
while (age.length == 0)
{
   age = prompt('You cannot leave this empty. What's your age?');
}


alert('Your age is ' + age + '. Got it!');


var password = prompt('Please enter your desired password: ');
while (password.length == 0)
{
   password = prompt('You cannot leave this empty. Please enter your desired password:');
}


alert('Your password is ' + password + '. Got it!');
```

Notice how the program now asks for input again and again until it gets a valid input from the user. Take note, however, that a repeated pop-up only serves as an example to illustrate the power of the while-loops and should not be used in actual programs, especially in websites; nobody likes receiving too much intrusive pop-ups.

## Do-While Loops

There are times wherein you want to make sure that a set of instructions get executed at least ONCE before possibly repeating, no matter what happens. For instance:

```
var bool = false;
while (bool)
{
    console.log("I wanna be seen!");
}
```

Because the condition already returns false, nothing inside the while loop gets executed. Do-while loops, on the other hand, has the following syntax:

```
do
{
```

```
    <something>
} while (<condition>);
```

Notice how the while statement goes at the end of the block of code, followed by a semicolon, because the computer checks for the condition only when the block of code inside the do-while loop has been executed. Modifying our previous example, we now have:

```
var bool = false;

do

{

console.log("I wanna be seen!");

} while (bool);
```

As an exercise, rewrite the example that asks for the user's name, email, age, and password to use do-while loops. Instead of saying "you cannot leave this empty...", you can instead ask the user "What's your..." again.

## If-Else If-Else

So far, we've only made if-else statements that only gave us two options to choose from - execute the block of code EITHER in the if or else statement. Fortunately, if we need to add more options, we can just add an 'else if' block between the if and else blocks. That being said, here's what the if-else if-else statement would look like:

```
if ( <condition> )
{
   <action>
}
else if ( <condition> )
{
   <action>
}
else
{
   <action>
}
```

Here's an example on how we can apply the if-else if-else statement:

```
var input = prompt("Please enter a number: ");


if(input.length == 0)

{

   alert("You haven't entered anything!");

}

else if(isNaN(input)) //isNaN is a function that checks if the data in question is a number or not. It actually stands for is-Not-a-Number.

{

   alert(input+" isn't a number!");

}

else

{

   alert("You've typed: " + input);

}
```

As an exercise, create a loop that will keep asking the user for a number until the user provides valid input (strings and empty input aren't valid). Hint: a combination of a do-while and an if-else if-else code would be useful.

## Switch Statement

If-else if-else statements let you give conditional instructions to the computer, but sometimes, one just needs the computer to perform specific instructions based on specific user input. The analogue of this in real life would be like choosing drinks from a vending machine. With set, hardwired choices, it wouldn't make sense to have the user type in his choice. It'd make more sense to have buttons that correspond to the preferred drink. With that in mind, here's what a switch statement would look like:

```
var drinks = ["[a] Soda", "[b] Juice", "[c] Water", "[d] Milk"];

var choice = prompt("Hi there! What are you in the mood for? We have: " + drinks + ". Please key in the letter of your choice.");


switch(choice)

{

  case 'a':

    alert("Dispensing one soda. Have a nice day!");

    break;

  case 'b':
```

```
        alert("Dispensing one juice. Have a nice day!");
        break;
    case 'c':
        alert("Dispensing one water. Have a nice day!");
        break;
    case 'd':
        alert("Dispensing one milk. Have a nice day!");
        break;
    case null:
        alert("You don't want anything? Alright, have a nice day!");
        break;
    case '':
        alert("You don't want anything? Alright, have a nice day!");
        break;
    default:
        alert("I've never heard of this " + choice + ". Here, take this water instead.");
}
```

Notice how it's really quite similar to the if-else if-else statement, except that you can't put mathematical expressions in the cases; you can only let the computer pick the block of code to execute based on the input the user gives. The 'default' block, much like the 'else' block, tells the computer what to do in case the user doesn't pick any of the choices that have corresponding cases in the switch statement.

Note: the 'break' keyword tells the computer that the code for the specific case is finished executing and therefore can exit the statement. If you remove this, the code continues to other cases; always remember to place a 'break' after every case!

## Review

Well done! You've just completed your arsenal of flow control tools:

1. The if-else and if-else if-else statements
2. The for, while, and do-while loops
3. The switch statement

It is by mastering these flow control tools that you can make more efficient programs, so it's important to keep practicing and look at new ways in which you can optimize your code better. For instance, let's take a look at our text-search application (take note of the added lines in red):

```
var textBlock = "And so we're back to this program.";
```

```
var queryWord = "so";


var matchCount = 0;


for (var counter = 0; counter < textBlock.length; counter++)
{
    console.log("Outer for loop now processing letter: " + textBlock[counter]);

   if((textBlock[counter] == queryWord[0]) && (textBlock.length-counter >= queryWord.length))
    {
     console.log("Code block inside 'if-else' statement now processing letter: " + textBlock[counter]);

     var match = true;

     for(var counter1 = 0; counter1 < queryWord.length; counter1++)
      {
        if(!(textBlock[counter+counter1]           ==
queryWord[counter1]))
         {
            match = false;
```

```
        break;

    }

}

    if(match==true)

    {

        matchCount++;

    }

}

else

{

    console.log("Code block inside 'if-else' statement now processing letter: " + textBlock[counter]);

}

}


console.log('Done! Total matches: ' + matchCount);
```

While the program currently works well, the problem is that the outer loop continues to run even if the remaining letters left of the huge block of text isn't big enough to match our query. You can see this because both the for-loop code and the if-else code still display the console message we've added. In programming, we make sure that our program runs as efficiently as possible, so let's add a bit of code to optimize our program:

```
var textBlock = "And so we're back to this program.";

var queryWord = "back";


var matchCount = 0;


for (var counter = 0; counter < textBlock.length; counter++)

{

    console.log("Outer for loop now processing letter: " + textBlock[counter]);

    if((textBlock[counter] == queryWord[0]) && (textBlock.length-counter >= queryWord.length))

    {

        console.log("Code block inside 'if-else' statement now processing letter: " + textBlock[counter]);

        var match = true;

        for(var counter1 = 0; counter1 < queryWord.length; counter1++)

        {
```

```
        if(!(textBlock[counter+counter1]          ==
queryWord[counter1]))

        {

            match = false;

            break;

        }

    }

    if(match==true)

    {

        matchCount++;

    }

}

else if(!(textBlock.length-counter >= queryWord.length))

{

    console.log("""                         +textBlock.substring(counter, textBlock.length) + """ + " is too small to match " + """ + queryWord + """);

    break;

}

else
```

```
    {
        console.log("Code block inside 'if-else' statement now processing letter: " + textBlock[counter]);
    }
}

console.log('Done! Total matches: ' + matchCount);
```

With this tiny modification, we get to stop the program from performing extra computations. While this might seem like a lot of trouble to go through just to prevent unnecessary loops from occurring, in more complex programs or in online applications that have to be perfectly responsive and light, we can't afford to have any 'leak' in system performance. Just make sure you don't get too carried away applying tiny tweaks if your program isn't even finished yet.

We've so far been fiddling with our mini text-search application, but there's actually a neat function that could help us shorten our code - the search() function. Let's try it out:

```
var text = "I've gone through all this trouble and it turns out there's an easy way out.";

var positionOfText = text.search("easy way out");

console.log(positionOfText);
```

Though take note that the search() function only looks for the location of the first occurrence of the query in the text. You can, however, modify the original program and use the search() function within the for loop to make the code shorter. This is another important lesson in programming - learning how to find the right function for the job so you won't end up writing one yourself. That being said, here's another way to achieve our mini text-search application using another function called "match()":

```
var text = "This is getting ridiculous.";

var results = text.match("ridiculous");

console.log("Matches: " + results.length);
```

What we've done before - creating the text-search app with only the basic if-else if-else and for-loops - helps us understand what happens inside the functions that we often take for granted. By understanding this, we could easily create our own functions in case the available ones don't fit our needs.

## Conclusion

So far, you pretty much now have the basic procedural parts of JavaScript covered. In the next chapter, you'll learn more about data structures, which is a way of organizing information (remember our lesson about arrays?) so that the computer can manage it more efficiently. If in the past few chapters, we've talked about general procedural programming concepts (if-else statements, functions, etc.) using JavaScript, the next chapter will help you get a running start on object-oriented programming concepts.

# Chapter 7: Managing Data More Efficiently

In this chapter, you'll learn how to manage data more efficiently by learning about data structures. You've already actually learned a data structure back in Chapter 5 - arrays. In this chapter, we'll explore arrays more thoroughly, as well as give you an introduction to objects, which are pretty much what separate object-oriented programming from procedural programming. With that said, let's have a quick review of arrays first:

## Arrays - A Quick Review

Here's a bunch of arrays:

```
var fruits = ["Banana", "Apple", "Orange"];

var numbers = [1, 2, 3];

var fruitSalad = ["Banana", "Apple", "Orange",1, 2, 3];
```

Arrays with two or more types of data are called heterogeneous arrays. In the above example, 'fruitSalad' is the heterogeneous array. You can store any kind of data type in an array and access it using the index of the corresponding data:

```
console.log(fruits[0]); //should give you Banana
```

```
console.log(fruitSalad[5]); //should give you 3
```

You can check the length of an array the same way you can with strings:

```
console.log(fruits.length); //should give you 3

console.log(numbers.length); //should give you 3

console.log(fruitSalad.length); //should give you 6
```

There are plenty of methods you can use on an array, like the push() method:

```
fruits.push("Tomato");
```

You can find a comprehensive list of methods for arrays with a quick online search, as adding them all here would make the book too dense.

Now that you've gotten a quick review of arrays, let's make things a little more interesting by talking about two-dimensional arrays.

## Two-Dimensional Arrays

When we've discussed arrays being able to keep any kind of data, we're not just talking about strings, numbers, and booleans; we can also store arrays in arrays! How is this useful? Well, let's say you were to save personal information in an array:

```
var personalInfo = ["John", 23, "johnSnow@myCorporation.net"];
```

What happens when you want to add more people, though? Just like what we do when we want to create a list of information, we also create a list of arrays:

```
var group = [personalInfo, ["Jen", 21, "jenRose@myCorporation.net"], ["Jake", 25, "jakeSullivan@myCorporation.net"]];
```

To recall our lesson in for-loops, let's iterate through each entry's personal information:

```
for(var counter = 0; counter < group.length; counter++)
{
  for(var counter1 = 0; counter1 < group[counter].length; counter1++)
  {
```

```
        console.log(group[counter][counter1]);
   }
}
```

Try to play around with this code a bit and try to present the data in reverse:

1. Display Jake's information first and John's information last

2. Display the email address first and the names last

Now that you've gotten the hand of two-dimensional arrays, it's time to jump into a higher plane - the plane of objects!

## Introduction to Objects

Procedural programming required programmers to spell out almost every command to the computer. This can quickly lead to messy code, so people thought about keeping certain commands and information inside what one can call an "object." For instance, if you wanted to create a database of pets, you'd have to do something like:

```
//First, we create arrays with the information we wish to save
var petName = ["Cat", "Spot", "Fluffy"];
var petSpecies = ["Dog", "Fish", "Parrot"];
var petAge = [5, 2, 6];
var petGender = ["Male", "Female", "Male"];
var petDetails = [petName, petSpecies, petAge, petGender];
//Then we create a function that displays them
var displayInformation = function(details)
{
   for(var counter = 0; counter < petSpecies.length; counter++)
   {
   console.log("Name: "+ details[0][counter]);
   console.log("Species: "+ details[1][counter]);
   console.log("Age: "+ details[2][counter]);
```

```
    console.log("Gender: "+ details[3][counter]);

  }

};



displayInformation(petDetails);
```

While the code does work and provides us with a relatively neat list of information, the code is rather messy and can get pretty hard to debug when new functions and details are added. That being said, here's a code snippet that turns the first entry into an object:

```
var pet = {};

pet.name = "Cat";

pet.species = "Dog";

pet.age = 5;

pet.gender = "Male";


pet.showDetails = function()

{

    console.log("Name: "+ this.name);
```

```
    console.log("Species: "+ this.species);

    console.log("Age: "+ this.age);

    console.log("Gender: "+ this.gender);
}



pet.showDetails();
```

This line:

```
var pet = {};
```

Is what creates an object with the name "pet." There are actually two ways to create an object, and this is the first, called the *literal notation*. We've started with an empty object and added attributes after the declaration, but we can actually start with a filled object:

```
var pet = {

   name: "Cat",

   species: "Dog",

   age: 5,

   gender: "Male",
```

```
};
```

```
pet.showDetails = function()
{
   console.log("Name: "+ this.name);
   console.log("Species: "+ this.species);
   console.log("Age: "+ this.age);
   console.log("Gender: "+ this.gender);
}


pet.showDetails();
```

Take note of the differences, subtle as they may be! (e.g., using a colon (:) instead of an equal sign (=))

You can also use a constructor, turning the code snippet into:

```
var pet = new Object();
pet.name = "Cat";
```

```
pet.species = "Dog";

pet.age = 5;

pet.gender = "Male";


pet.showDetails = function()
{
   console.log("Name: "+ this.name);
   console.log("Species: "+ this.species);
   console.log("Age: "+ this.age);
   console.log("Gender: "+ this.gender);
}


pet.showDetails();
```

Both ways of creating objects are correct, so it really is all up to preference.

Now notice how the object is a little bit different from the other data types we've used so far. This is because objects are modern concepts that serve to represent real world stuff by keeping all the relevant details and information in one place. For instance, if one is to create a "phone" object, then it'd most likely contain attributes like screen size, pixel density, number and speed of processors, RAM, etc. If we want to create different phones, we'd just simply have to do something like:

```
var smartPhone1 = {
  screenSize: 5,
  pixelDensity: 200,
  processorNumber: 2,
  processorSpeed: 500,
};
var smartPhone2 = {
  screenSize: 6,
  pixelDensity: 400,
  processorNumber: 8,
  processorSpeed: 2000,
};
```

This makes organizing data much more efficient and easy.

As an exercise, print out the details of each phone into the console by accessing the properties using the dot notation. To start you off, here's the code for the screenSize of smartPhone1 printed to the console:

```
console.log(smartPhone1.screenSize);
```

So far, we can access either information or functions of an object using the dot notation. The variables we access using the dot notation are called *properties*, while the functions we access using the dot notation are called *methods*.

The concept of methods and properties arose from the need to turn real life concepts into code. Going back to our phone example, for instance, without objects there's no simple way to tell which screen size belongs to a specific phone, unless one keeps the phone names and screen sizes in two different arrays. This quickly becomes more complicated when more attributes are added.

Going back to our explanations about functions, functions are able to keep a large number of instructions without messing up the whole source code by being invokable with a function name. Going back to our phone example, phones differ in terms of what functionalities are available, as well as the internal implementation of those functionalities. For instance, let's add a texting function to the two phones from our example earlier, as well as the capability to swap sim cards:

```
var smartPhone1 = {
  screenSize: 5,
```

```
    pixelDensity: 200,

    processorNumber: 2,

    processorSpeed: 500,

    simCardNumber: 123456,


    textNumber: function(number, text)
    {
        console.log("Message, '" + text + "' has been sent to " + number);
        console.log("Processing time: " + text.length/this.processorNumber);
    },


    setSimCardNumber: function(newSimCardNumber)
    {
        this.simCardNumber = newSimCardNumber;
    },
};
var smartPhone2 = {
```

```
    screenSize: 6,

    pixelDensity: 400,

    processorNumber: 8,

    processorSpeed: 2000,

    simCardNumber: 654321,


    textNumber: function(number, text)
    {
        console.log("'" + text + "' sent to " + number);
        console.log("Processing time:       " + text.length/this.processorNumber);
    },


    setSimCardNumber: function(newSimCardNumber)
    {
        this.simCardNumber = newSimCardNumber;
    },
};
```

Notice how both phones have the same set of functions, but with a slightly different implementation, just as in real life, when you tell somebody to text someone, you only need to specify the message and the number you need to send it to regardless of the type of phone used. As for the setSimCardNumber function, this is actually common practice in object-oriented programming; instead of setting the properties of an object manually, like:

```
smartPhone1.simCardNumber = 55555;
```

Since the setter at least can have an extra set of instructions, like checking for any possible errors in the process.

Another thing you might have noticed is that we're using the keyword, "this" when we're creating methods for our objects. The keyword, "this" acts as a placeholder and will point to the object that called the method. For example, if you type:

```
smartPhone2.textNumber(0000, "Hi!");
```

Then we call the function:

```
textNumber: function(number, text)
{
    console.log("'" + text + "' sent to " + number);
    console.log("Processing     time:     "     + text.length/this.processorNumber);
```

```
},
```

This makes references to a processorNumber variable. Because of the "this" keyword, the function finds a variable called "processorNumber" in the object that called it, which is "smartPhone2."

## Custom Constructors

As you may have noticed, having to create and assign properties every time for similar objects is quite a hassle. Since smartPhone1 and smartPhone2 are both classified as phones, then they're bound to have similar methods and properties. With that in mind, we can do something like this to make our code cleaner:

```
function   Phone(screenSize, pixelDensity,   processorNumber, processorSpeed, simCardNumber)
{
    this.screenSize = screenSize;

    this.pixelDensity = pixelDensity;

    this.processorNumber = processorNumber;

    this.processorSpeed = processorSpeed;

    this.simCardNumber = simCardNumber;
```

```
    this.textNumber = function(number, text)
    {
        console.log("'" + text + "' sent to " + number);
        console.log("Processing       time:       "       +  text.length/this.processorNumber);
    };


    this.setSimCardNumber = function(newSimCardNumber)
    {
        this.simCardNumber = newSimCardNumber;
    };

}
```

//Now we can create our two smart phones using the constructor we've just made!

var smartPhone1 = new Phone(5, 200, 2, 500, 123456);

var smartPhone2 = new Phone(6, 400, 8, 2000, 654321);

```
//let's add a new phone!

var simplePhone1 = new Phone(2.5, 100, 1, 80, 111111);
```

See how it makes our code much shorter? In real life, this would be the equivalent of creating a factory - you systemize the creation of objects while allowing a certain number of customizations to be made after the basics are taken care of.

## Conclusion

Congratulations! You've just had your first exposure to object-oriented programming! Object-oriented programming lets you create code that's much easier to understand at first glance because of the concepts of properties and methods. Knowing how to create and manipulate objects is the first step, just as learning the syntax for procedural programming is also the first step. The second step is learning how to break down complex problems into chunks of code, and in object-oriented programming, it means learning how to represent data as objects. In the final chapter, we'll take a deeper exploration into the realm of object-oriented programming so that you can get a better sense of how we can take advantage of objects.

# Chapter 8: Exploring Objects

So far, we've talked about how one can create objects to make it easier to break down complex problems, as well as represent real-life concepts in JavaScript. In this chapter, you'll learn a little more about how you can identify objects, as well as how you can run through their properties. To cap things off, we'll then talk about some important object-oriented concepts to help you get started on your journey to more complicated object-oriented programming concepts, the scope of which lies outside this book.

## Identifying Data Types

With bigger code come more chances of messing up and forgetting the data type one's dealing with. Furthermore, some hackers may also take advantage of unchecked data types to exploit a possible security hole in the JavaScript app. That being said, in order to find out what the data type of the information you're dealing with is, simply use the *typeof* keyword. For example:

```
var numberSample = 12;

var stringSample = "AAA";

var objectSample = { property1: "Sample string" };

console.log("Type of numberSample is: "+ typeof
```

```
numberSample);

console.log("Type of stringSample is: "+ typeof stringSample);

console.log("Type of objectSample is: "+ typeof objectSample);
```

## Distinguishing Between Different Objects

We now know how to identify strings, numbers, and objects, but since objects have an inner classification (an object of type Phone is different from an object of type Car, for instance), it's a good idea to be able to distinguish between different objects too. Unfortunately, JavaScript provides no built-in way to provide you with the type of the object you're dealing with. You can, however, confirm if you're dealing with a specific type of object. Take this sample code, for instance:

```
function Vehicle(transmission, color, type)
{
    this.transmission = transmission;
    this.color = color;
    this.type = type;
}


function Boat(type, color)
```

```
{
    this.type = type;
    this.color = color;
}
var blueTruck = new Vehicle("automatic", "blue", "truck");
var greenBoat = new Boat("sailboat", "green");
```

We can use the following code to check if blueTruck and greenBoat are vehicles or boats:

```
console.log("Is blueTruck a vehicle? " + (blueTruck instanceof Vehicle));
console.log("Is greenBoat a vehicle? " + (greenBoat instanceof Vehicle));
console.log("Is blueTruck a boat? " + (blueTruck instanceof Boat));
console.log("Is greenBoat a boat? " + (greenBoat instanceof Boat));
```

## Data Verification

In programming, it's always important to verify the data you're dealing with, especially since the computer can easily go haywire when fed with information it doesn't expect. That being said, just as it's important to verify the object you're dealing with in certain cases, it's also important to verify the existence of methods you're using.

In smaller codes, this might not be too important since it's relatively easy to keep track of methods and objects in your code, but in cases wherein you're tasked to build and maintain a complex program, certain methods could be updated or removed in newer versions of the program. That being said, it's a good idea to check the availability of methods and properties that you suspect may change in the future. Here's a sample code that helps you determine whether a method or property exists in an object:

```
//Sample function
function Sample(aNumber, aString)
{
    this.aNumber = aNumber;
    this.aString = aString;
    this.aFunction = function()
    {
        console.log("This is a function");
```

```
  };
}
//Method and Property check
var newObject = new Sample(0, "Hello");


console.log("Testing if aFunction exists: " + (typeof newObject.aFunction == 'function'));

console.log("Testing if anotherFunction exists: " + (typeof newObject.anotherFunction == 'function'));


console.log("Testing if aNumber exists: " + newObject.hasOwnProperty("aNumber"));

console.log("Testing if anotherNumber exists: " + newObject.hasOwnProperty("anotherNumber"));
```

In this code, we've used the 'typeof' keyword to check whether a certain function exists inside a method. If the method doesn't exist, the statement should return false, otherwise, it returns true. We've then introduced a new method called *hasOwnProperty()* to check whether a property exists in an object or not. As an exercise, do the same type of testing for the 'aString' variable.

# Running through properties in a loop

Surprisingly, there's a variation of the for-loop in JavaScript that you can use to run through all the properties of a method. This modified for-loop is called a for-in loop, and it looks like this:

```
var sampleObject =
{
   name: "John Smith",
   age: 22,
   job: "Software Engineer",
};


for(var property in sampleObject)
{
   console.log(property);
}
```

This type of for-loop is usually only available in object-oriented programming languages because it hides a lot of lines of code that allow you to run through each property inside an object without creating an intricate for-loop with counters and iterations.

## Conclusion

Object-oriented programming contains a lot of new concepts that may baffle people who are used to using procedural languages like C. Some of these include:

- Inheritance - getting properties and methods from the parent class. You've seen this happen whenever you call on functions and properties of an object you've created from a parent class.

- Polymorphism - allows you to replace methods previously defined in the prototype class, e.g.,

```
function Sample(firstNumber, secondNumber)
{
  this.firstNumber = firstNumber;
  this.secondNumber = secondNumber;
  this.sampleFunction = function()
  {
    console.log(this.firstNumber + this.secondNumber);
  };
}

var functionA = new Sample(5, 10);
```

```
var functionB = new Sample(5, 10);

//In here, we've redefined the sampleFunction() method, but only for functionB:

functionB.sampleFunction = function()
{
  console.log(this.firstNumber - this.secondNumber);
};

//Notice how functionB now does things differently from functionA even though they both come from the same class, which is Sample.

functionA.sampleFunction();

functionB.sampleFunction();
```

- Prototype Changes - changing the prototype class so that we can add new functions that all the objects under that class can use, e.g.,

```
function Sample (aNumber)
{
  this.aNumber = aNumber;
}
```

```
var objectFromSample = new Sample(15);

//Here, we add a new property using the 'prototype' keyword

Sample.prototype.aString = "Hi there!";

console.log(objectFromSample.aString);

var anotherObjectFromSample = new Sample(25);

console.log(anotherObjectFromSample.aString);
```

With the power to create many instances of objects, you can create all kinds of applications, from games that rely on multiple instances of enemies, weapons, etc., to web applications that rely on multiple data from users. It is through practice that one learns how to use them efficiently. Hopefully, this chapter has introduced enough of the object-oriented programming concepts to get you going.

# Conclusion

Congratulations! You are now ready to explore JavaScript on your own; you can check out other people's codes and see how they work, or search for more JavaScript methods and other information available online. While JavaScript has been known as the interactive language of the web, more and more developers are now discovering how JavaScript can be used in other platforms, like Android and iOS. There are plenty of resources online that can help you use JavaScript in mobile development and web development, but hopefully this book has given you a head start in the concepts of programming.

JavaScript is just one of the many languages out there; if you're interested in web programming, I suggest you pick up a book on HTML5 and CSS. If you're interested in mobile development, I suggest you pick up a book on Android development or iOS Development (make sure you get a fairly recent copy for iOS development, since the language used for older iOS versions is different).

Remember that your learning doesn't stop when you flip the last page; in fact, it is after the last page of the book that you get to test your book knowledge and gain experiential knowledge. Keep in mind that programming, more than a hobby or a job, is a lifestyle. Programmers take it upon themselves to solve the problems people don't see. They create problems, and then they solve them. They train themselves to find what can be improved, from unresponsive webpages, to boring websites, to the creation of cross platform apps.

I wish you the best of luck!

*Robert Dwight*

Made in the USA
Middletown, DE
21 August 2016